My First Book Animal Alphabet of the Philippines

Amazing Animal Books
Children's Picture Books

By Molly Davidson

Mendon Cottage Books

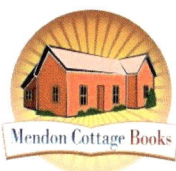

JD-Biz Publishing

Read More Amazing Animal Books

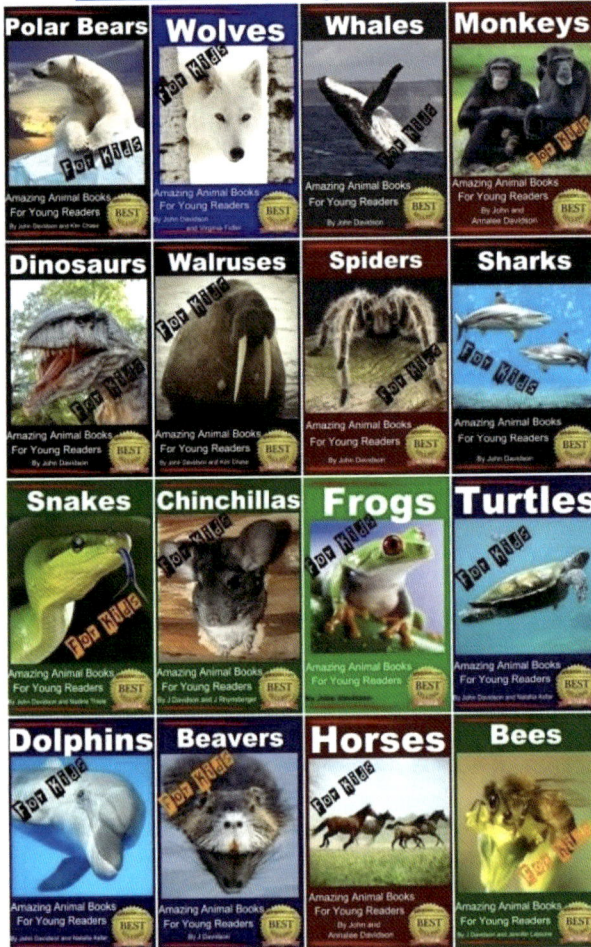

Purchase at Amazon.com

Download Free Books!
http://MendonCottageBooks.com

Introduction

The Philippines is a group of more than 7,000 islands off the coast of Southeast Asia.

They have many interesting and exclusive animals living off the coast and on land.

Let's read some more about a few of these amazing animals.

Be on the lookout for bonus letters, some letters have more than one animal!

A is for an Asian Elephant.

Asian elephants are smaller than African elephants, but they still weigh about 2 - 5 1/2 ton (2,000 - 5,000 kg).

B is for a Bamboo Bat.

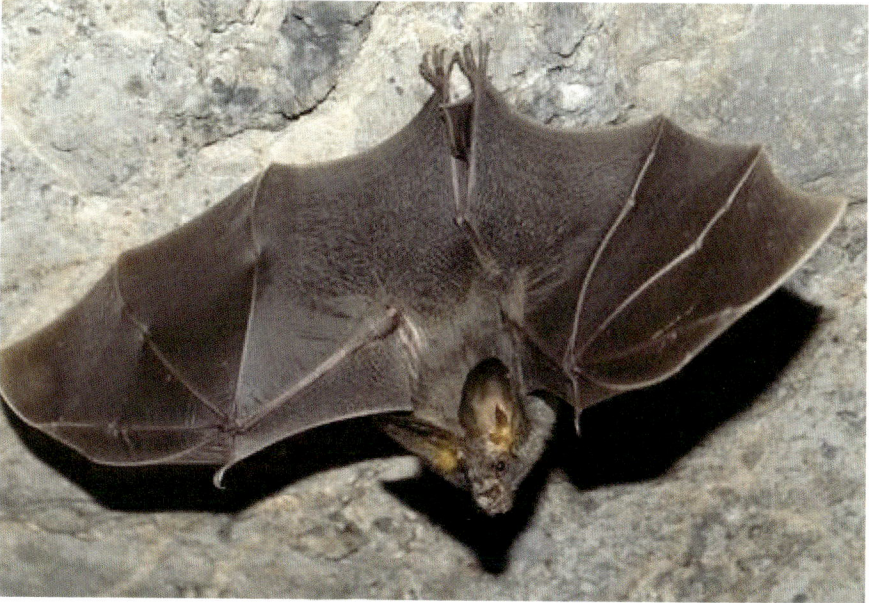

The bamboo bat is one of the smallest mammals in the World; it is about the size of a bumble bee!

They live in the hollow shoots of giant bamboo, which helps protect them from predators, since most animals are too large to fit inside.

C is for a Crab-Eating Macaque.

The crab-eating macaque is also called the long-tailed macaque, due to the fact that its tail is usually longer than its body.

D is for a Dugong.

The dugong is a relative of the manatee and the elephant, even though they have very similar characteristics to a whale.

They live about 70 years in the wild, eating any and all ocean vegetation.

D is also for a Pantropical Spotted Dolphin.

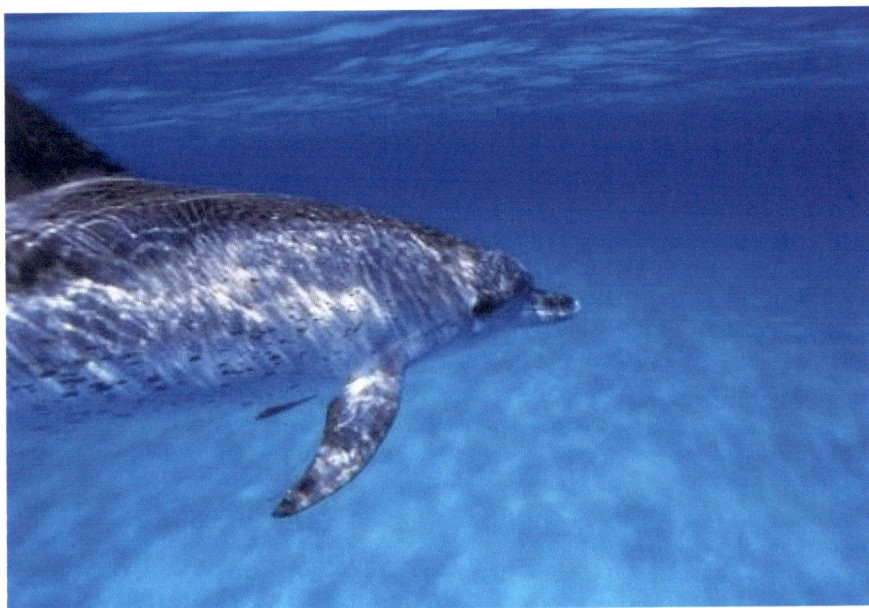

Pantropical spotted dolphins do not get their spots until they are an adult, which is usually when they are about 10 - 12 years old.

They like to swim in warm shallow waters, which are abundant around the Philippines.

E is for a Filipino Eagle.

The Filipino eagle is the National bird of the Philippines.

They are one of the longest of all the eagles in the World, stretching out to about 3 1/2 feet (102 cm).

F is for a Freshwater Crocodile.

In the Philippines the freshwater crocodile is called "Buwaya."

They lay between 7 - 20 eggs, which take about 3 months to hatch.

They have 66 - 68 teeth that are continually falling out, and new ones are replacing them.

G is for a Dwarf Pygmy Goby.

The dwarf pygmy goby is one of the smallest freshwater fish, only measuring about 1.5 cm long.

They are called "bia" or "tabios" by the Filipinos.

H is for a Humpback Whale.

Humpback whales are about the length of a school bus and weigh about 40 ton.

They are very powerful swimmers; they use their back tail fin, called a fluke, to push themselves out of the water.

I is for an Intermediate Egret.

Intermediate egrets live in shallow coastal or fresh water, where they eat frogs, crustaceans, fish, and insects.

It only stands about 28 inches (72 cm) tall, but it has a wingspan of 45 inches (115 cm).

J is for a Javan Pangolin.

Javan pangolins live in the trees of dense forests.

They have rough pads on the bottom of their feet, used for climbing, as well as sharp claws to dig up the dirt hills of termites.

K is for a Katanglad Shrew Mouse.

There have been only a few Katanglad shrew mice ever seen, they can only be found on Mount Katanglad in the Philippines.

Shrews are very territorial and will fight for their space, they only come together to mate.

L is for a Flying Lemur.

Flying lemurs don't really fly; they just spread out their arms and legs, which spread out a skin membrane, and then they jump from tree to tree, gliding through the air.

In the Philippines they are called "Kagwangs."

M is for a Magellan Birdwing Butterfly.

Robert Nash © Wikimedia Commons

This large butterfly is named after Ferdinand Magellan, the explorer, who was killed in the Philippines in 1521.

N is for a Naja, the scientific name for a Cobra.

The Philippines cobra is also called "Ulopong," and is one of the top 10 most venomous snakes in the World.

Cobras can live up to 20 years in the wild.

O

is for a Lesser Eagle Owl.

The lesser eagle owl can only be found on the islands of the Philippines.

They have three sets of eyelids.

They hunt small mammals and insects, usually at night.

P is for a Palawan Bearcat.

Palawan bearcats hunt at night and sleep on tree branches, in the forest, during the day.

They are considered an adult when they are 2 years old, and have between 2 - 6 babies after each mating season.

P is also for a Parrot.

The most common parrot found in the tropical jungles of the Philippines is the cockatoo (pictured above).

R is for a Rufous Hornbill.

The rufous hornbill, also called the "Kalaw," is a large bird only found in the Philippines.

S is for a Sailfin Lizard.

The sailfin lizard is about 3 feet (1 m) long, and they only live on the islands of the Philippines.

They are very quick runners, and will spread their toes out and run across the top of the water.

T is for a Tamaraw.

The tamaraw, an almost extinct type of water buffalo, can only be found on the Filipino island of Mindoro.

The boys' horns are longer and stronger than the girls, some measuring up to 20 inches (51 cm).

T is also for a Tarsier.

Tarsiers are small monkeys that have eyes that are larger than their brain!

Their strong back legs let them jump about 16 ft (5 m) from tree to tree.

U

U **is for a Urogale Everetti, the scientific name for a Mindanao Tree Shrew.**

Shreeram M V © Wikimedia Commons

The Mindanao tree shrew lives in the forests of the Filipino island of Mindanao.

They are very quick climbers and runners on the ground.

V

is for a Visayan Warty Pig.

The Visayan warty hog is only found on the islands of the Philippines.

They eat root vegetables, tubulars, and fruit found in the dense forests and woodlands.

W is for a Whale Shark, called a Butanding.

The whale shark is the largest fish in the World, measuring as long as 65 1/2 (20 m).

They have hundreds of tiny teeth that they use to eat zooplankton, small fish, squid, and crustaceans.

X is for a Xenus Cinereus, the scientific name for a Terek Sandpiper.

Terek sandpipers use a high whistle as a call.

They like to eat insects, but will usually first run to the water's edge to rinse them off before eating them.

Y

is for a Yellow Bittern.

Yellow bitterns are small birds, standing about 15 inches (38 cm) tall.

They will lay 4 to 6 eggs in the reed beds along the water's edge, hidden in the shrubs for protection.

Z is a Zambales Forest Mouse.

They were only discovered by a team of scientists lead by L.R. Heaney in 2000.

The Zambales forest mouse is one of the smallest in their subgenus.

Horses
For Kids
Amazing Animal Books
For Young Readers
By John and
Annalee Davidson

Ponies
For Kids
Mendon Cottage Books
AmazingAnimalBooks
For Young Readers
Rachel Smith

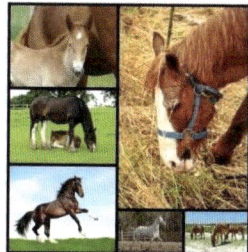

Ten Amazing Horses For Kids
Nature Books for Kids
JD-Biz Publishing
K. Bennett

Akhal-Teke
"The Golden Horse of the desert"
For Kids
Nature Books for Kids
JD-Biz Publishing
K. Bennett

Suffolk-Punch
"The Gentle Giant"
For Kids
Nature Books for Kids
JD-Biz Publishing
K. Bennett

Shires
"The great Horse"
For Kids
Nature Books for Kids
JD-Biz Publishing
K. Bennett

Colonial Spanish
"Horse of the Americas"
For Kids
Nature Books for Kids
JD-Biz Publishing
K. Bennett

Canadian
"The Little Iron Horse"
For Kids
Nature Books for Kids
JD-Biz Publishing
K. Bennett

Cleveland Bays
"History and Future"
Horses For Kids
Nature Books for Kids
JD-Biz Publishing
K. Bennett

Dinosaurs For Kids — Amazing Animal Books For Young Readers — By John Davidson

Ankylosaurus The Armored Dinosaur — Dinosaur Books For Young Readers — Enrique Fiesta

Tyrannosaurus Rex For Kids — Amazing Animal Books For Young Readers — Enrique Fiesta & John Davidson

Apatosaurus The Thunder Lizard — Dinosaur Books For Young Readers — Enrique Fiesta and John Davidson

Archaeopteryx Ancient Wings — Dinosaur Books For Young Readers — Enrique Fiesta and John Davidson

Smilodon Saber-toothed Tiger — Dinosaur Books For Young Readers — Enrique Fiesta

Pterosaurs The Flying Reptiles — Dinosaur Books For Young Readers — Enrique Fiesta

Dilophosaurus The Two-Crested Dinosaur — Dinosaur Books For Young Readers — Enrique Fiesta

Introduction to Dinosaurs — Dinosaur Books For Young Readers — Enrique Fiesta

Allosaurus The Strange Reptile — Dinosaur Books For Young Readers — Enrique Fiesta

Dimetrodon Permian Predator — Dinosaur Books For Young Readers — Enrique Fiesta

Triceratops The Three-Horned Dinosaur — Dinosaur Books For Young Readers — Enrique Fiesta

Spinosaurus The Spine Reptile — Dinosaur Books For Young Readers — Enrique Fiesta

Megalodon The Mega Shark! — Dinosaur Books For Young Readers — Enrique Fiesta

Pachycephalosaurus Thick-Headed Lizard — Dinosaur Books For Young Readers — Enrique Fiesta

Parasaurolophus The Crested Reptile — Dinosaur Books For Young Readers — Enrique Fiesta

Sarcosuchus King Crocodile — Dinosaur Books For Young Readers — Enrique Fiesta

Stegosaurus The Dinosaur with a Roof — Dinosaur Books For Young Readers — Enrique Fiesta

Troodon The Wounding Tooth — Dinosaur Books For Young Readers — Enrique Fiesta

Tylosaurus Predator of the Deep — Dinosaur Books For Young Readers — Enrique Fiesta

Crocodiles For Kids — Amazing Animal Books For Young Readers — Zahra Jazeel & John Davidson

Carnataurus The Horned Predator — Dinosaur Books For Young Readers — Enrique Fiesta

Salamanders For Kids — Amazing Animal Books — Zahra Jazeel and John Davidson

Crocodilians For Kids — Amazing Animal Books — Rachel Smith

Lizards For Kids — Amazing Animal Books — Rachel Smith

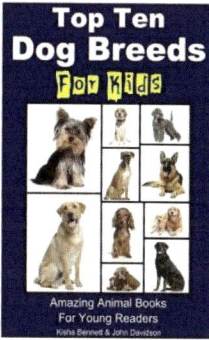

Top Ten Dog Breeds For Kids

Amazing Animal Books For Young Readers

Kisha Bennett & John Davidson

German Shepherds

Dog Books for Kids
K. Bennett

Bulldogs

Dog Books for Kids
K. Bennett

Dachshund

Dog Books for Kids
K. Bennett

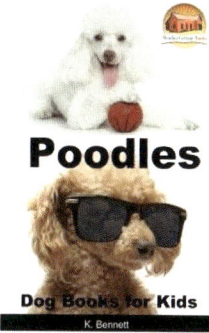

Poodles

Dog Books for Kids
K. Bennett

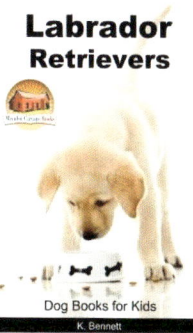

Labrador Retrievers

Dog Books for Kids
K. Bennett

Rottweilers

Dog Books for Kids
K. Bennett

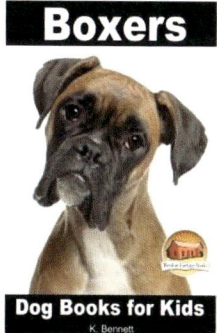

Boxers

Dog Books for Kids
K. Bennett

Golden Retrievers

Dog Books for Kids
K. Bennett

Puppies

Dog Books For Kids

Amazing Animal Books
For Young Readers

By John Davidson

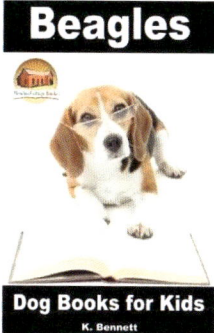

Beagles

Dog Books for Kids
K. Bennett

Yorkshire Terriers

Dog Books for Kids
K. Bennett

Dogs
Top Ten Dog Breeds **For Kids**

Amazing Animal Books For Young Readers

Zahra Jazeel & John Davidson

Cats For Kids

Amazing Animal Books For Young Readers

K. Bennett & John Davidson

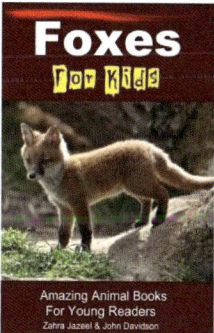

Foxes For Kids

Amazing Animal Books For Young Readers

Zahra Jazeel & John Davidson

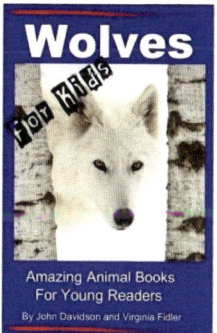

Wolves For Kids

Amazing Animal Books For Young Readers

By John Davidson and Virginia Fidler

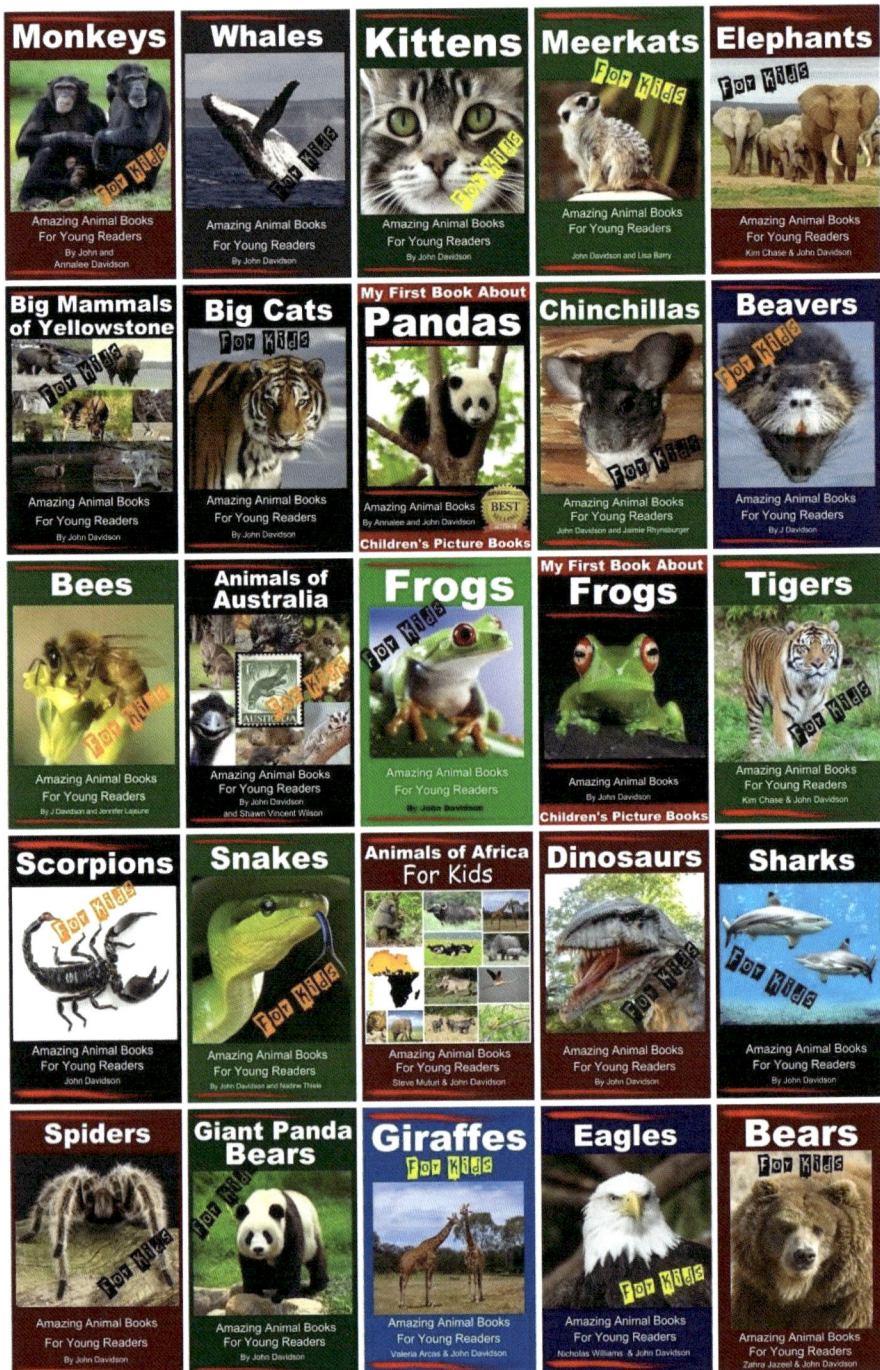

Monkeys
Amazing Animal Books
For Young Readers
By John and Annalee Davidson

Whales
Amazing Animal Books
For Young Readers
By John Davidson

Kittens
Amazing Animal Books
For Young Readers
By John Davidson

Meerkats
For Kids
Amazing Animal Books
For Young Readers
John Davidson and Lisa Barry

Elephants
For Kids
Amazing Animal Books
For Young Readers
Kim Chase & John Davidson

Big Mammals of Yellowstone
For Kids
Amazing Animal Books
For Young Readers
By John Davidson

Big Cats
For Kids
Amazing Animal Books
For Young Readers
By John Davidson

My First Book About
Pandas
Amazing Animal Books
By Annalee and John Davidson
BEST
Children's Picture Books

Chinchillas
Amazing Animal Books
For Young Readers
John Davidson and Jaimie Rhynsburger

Beavers
For Kids
Amazing Animal Books
For Young Readers
By J Davidson

Bees
Amazing Animal Books
For Young Readers
By J Davidson and Jennifer Lajeune

Animals of Australia
For Kids
Amazing Animal Books
For Young Readers
By John Davidson and Shawn Vincent Wilson

Frogs
For Kids
Amazing Animal Books
For Young Readers
By John Davidson

My First Book About
Frogs
Amazing Animal Books
By John Davidson
Children's Picture Books

Tigers
For Kids
Amazing Animal Books
For Young Readers
Kim Chase & John Davidson

Scorpions
For Kids
Amazing Animal Books
For Young Readers
John Davidson

Snakes
For Kids
Amazing Animal Books
For Young Readers
By John Davidson and Nadine Thiele

Animals of Africa
For Kids
Amazing Animal Books
For Young Readers
Steve Muturi & John Davidson

Dinosaurs
For Kids
Amazing Animal Books
For Young Readers
By John Davidson

Sharks
For Kids
Amazing Animal Books
For Young Readers
By John Davidson

Spiders
For Kids
Amazing Animal Books
For Young Readers
By John Davidson

Giant Panda Bears
For Kids
Amazing Animal Books
For Young Readers
By John Davidson

Giraffes
For Kids
Amazing Animal Books
For Young Readers
Valeria Arcas & John Davidson

Eagles
For Kids
Amazing Animal Books
For Young Readers
Nicholas Williams & John Davidson

Bears
For Kids
Amazing Animal Books
For Young Readers
Zahra Jazeel & John Davidson

Our books are available at

1. Amazon.com

2. Barnes and Noble

3. Itunes

4. Kobo

5. Smashwords

6. Google Play Books

Download Free Books!
http://MendonCottageBooks.com

Publisher

JD-Biz Corp

P O Box 374

Mendon, Utah 84325

http://www.jd-biz.com/

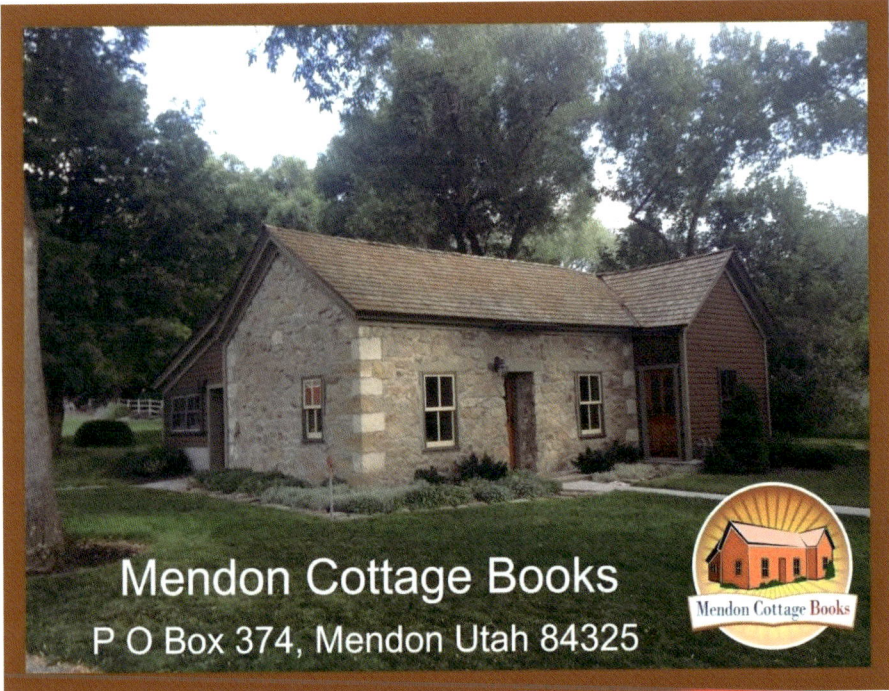

Mendon Cottage Books

P O Box 374, Mendon Utah 84325

CPSIA information can be obtained at www.ICGtesting.com
Printed in the USA
LVIW01n1136131116
512787LV00002B/6